THE COUNTRY BETWEEN US

CAROLYN FORCHÉ

THE COUNTRY BETWEEN US

1817

HARPER & ROW, PUBLISHERS, New York

Cambridge, Philadelphia, San Francisco, London,
Mexico City, São Paulo, Sydney

This book was designed by Sam Hamill at Copper Canyon Press
and is photographically reproduced from the signed, limited edition
published in December 1981.

FIRST HARPER & ROW EDITION

LIBRARY OF CONGRESS CATALOG CARD NUMBER: 81-47788
ISBN 0-06-014955-8   82 83 84 85 86 10 9 8 7 6 5 4 3 2 1
ISBN 0-06-090926-9 (pbk)   82 83 84 85 86 10 9 8 7 6 5 4 3 2 1

Some of these poems appeared previously as follows:
The American Poetry Review: As Children Together, Return, Reunion
Antaeus: Departure, Photograph of My Room
The Atlantic Monthly: Letter From Prague 1968–78, The Visitor
The New Yorker: For the Stranger (© 1978 The New Yorker)
Parnassus: The Memory of Elena
Pequod: Joseph; The Colonel; City Walk-Up, Winter 1969
The Virginia Quarterly Review: The Island; San Onofre, California
Anthology of Magazine Verse: *Yearbook of American Poetry*: Departure
Poet's Choice: Reunion
Women's International Resource Exchange: San Onofre, California; The Visitor;
    The Memory of Elena; The Island; The Colonel; Return
The Pushcart Prize VI: *Best of the Small Presses*: Return

I wish to thank the John Simon Guggenheim Memorial Foundation and the
National Endowment for the Arts for fellowships which enabled me to
complete this work.
I would also like to express my gratitude to Dara and Allen Wier,
Leonel Gómez Vides and those who remain in El Salvador.

FOR JAMES AND
FOR CUZCATLÁN

CONTENTS

IN SALVADOR, 1978–80

In memory of Monsignor Oscar Romero

Caminante, no hay camino
Se hace camino al andar.

ANTONIO MACHADO

SAN ONOFRE, CALIFORNIA

WE have come far south.
Beyond here, the oldest women
shelling limas into black shawls.
Portillo scratching his name
on the walls, the slender ribbons
of piss, children patting the mud.
If we go on, we might stop
in the street in the very place
where someone disappeared
and the words Come with us! we might
hear them. If that happened, we would
lead our lives with our hands
tied together. That is why we feel
it is enough to listen
to the wind jostling lemons,
to dogs ticking across the terraces,
knowing that while birds and warmer weather
are forever moving north,
the cries of those who vanish
might take years to get here.

1977

THE ISLAND

FOR CLARIBEL ALEGRÍA

I

In Deya when the mist
rises out of the rocks it comes
so close to her hands she could
tear it to pieces like bread.
She holds her drink and motions
with one hand to describe this:
what she would do with so many
baskets of bread.

Mi prieta, Asturias called her,
my dark little one. Neruda
used the word *negrita*, and it is
true: her eyes, her hair,
both violent, as black
as certain mornings have been
for the last fourteen years.
She wears a white cotton dress.
Tiny mirrors have been stitched
to it—when I look for myself
in her, I see the same face
over and over.

I have the fatty eyelids
of a Slavic factory girl,
the pale hair of mixed blood.
Although José Martí has said

we have lived our lives in the heart
of the beast, I have never heard
it pounding. When I have seen
an animal, I have never reached
for a knife. It is like
Americans to say it is only a bear
looking for something to eat
in the garbage.

But we are not unalike.
When we look at someone, we are seeing
someone else. When we listen
we hear something taking place
in the past. When I talk to her
I know what I will be saying
twenty years from now.

2
Last summer she returned
to Salvador again. It had been
ten years since *Ashes of Izalco*
was burned in a public place,
ten years without bushes
of coffee, since her eyes
crossed the finca like black
scattering birds.

It was simple. She was
there to embrace her mother.
As she walked through her village
the sight of her opened its windows.
It was simple. She had come
to flesh out the memory of a poet
whose body was never found.

Had it changed? It was different.
In Salvador nothing is changed.

3
Deya? A cluster of the teeth,
the bones of the world, greener
than Corsica. In English
you have no word for this. I can't
help you. I am safe here. I have
everything I could want.
In the morning I watch the peak
of the Teix knife into the clouds.
To my country I ship poetry instead
of bread, so I cut through nothing.
I give nothing, so you see I have
nothing, according to myself.

Deya has seven different shawls
of wind. The sky holds them
out to her, helps her into them.
I am *xaloc*, a wind
from the southwest as far away
as my country and there is nothing
to help me in or out of it.

Carolina, do you know how long it takes
any one voice to reach another?

1976-78

THE MEMORY OF ELENA

WE spend our morning
in the flower stalls counting
the dark tongues of bells
that hang from ropes waiting
for the silence of an hour.
We find a table, ask for *paella*,
cold soup and wine, where a calm
light trembles years behind us.

In Buenos Aires only three
years ago, it was the last time his hand
slipped into her dress, with pearls
cooling her throat and bells like
these, chipping at the night—

As she talks, the hollow
clopping of a horse, the sound
of bones touched together.
The *paella* comes, a bed of rice
and *camarones*, fingers and shells,
the lips of those whose lips
have been removed, mussels
the soft blue of a leg socket.

This is not *paella*, this is what
has become of those who remained
in Buenos Aires. This is the ring
of a rifle report on the stones,

her hand over her mouth,
her husband falling against her.

These are the flowers we bought
this morning, the dahlias tossed
on his grave and bells
waiting with their tongues cut out
for this particular silence.

1977

THE VISITOR

In Spanish he whispers there is no time left.
It is the sound of scythes arcing in wheat,
the ache of some field song in Salvador.
The wind along the prison, cautious
as Francisco's hands on the inside, touching
the walls as he walks, it is his wife's breath
slipping into his cell each night while he
imagines his hand to be hers. It is a small country.

There is nothing one man will not do to another.

1979

THE COLONEL

WHAT YOU HAVE HEARD is true. I was in his house. His wife carried a tray of coffee and sugar. His daughter filed her nails, his son went out for the night. There were daily papers, pet dogs, a pistol on the cushion beside him. The moon swung bare on its black cord over the house. On the television was a cop show. It was in English. Broken bottles were embedded in the walls around the house to scoop the kneecaps from a man's legs or cut his hands to lace. On the windows there were gratings like those in liquor stores. We had dinner, rack of lamb, good wine, a gold bell was on the table for calling the maid. The maid brought green mangoes, salt, a type of bread. I was asked how I enjoyed the country. There was a brief commercial in Spanish. His wife took everything away. There was some talk then of how difficult it had become to govern. The parrot said hello on the terrace. The colonel told it to shut up, and pushed himself from the table. My friend said to me with his eyes: say nothing. The colonel returned with a sack used to bring groceries home. He spilled many human ears on the table. They were like dried peach halves. There is no other way to say this. He took one of them in his hands, shook it in our faces, dropped it into a water glass. It came alive there. I am tired of fooling around he said. As for the rights of anyone, tell your people they can go fuck themselves. He swept the ears to the floor with his arm and held the last of his wine in the air. Something for your poetry, no? he said. Some of the ears on the floor caught this scrap of his voice. Some of the ears on the floor were pressed to the ground.

May 1978

RETURN

FOR JOSEPHINE CRUM

UPON my return to America, Josephine:
the iced drinks and paper umbrellas, clean
toilets and Los Angeles palm trees moving
like lean women, I was afraid more than
I had been, even of motels so much so
that for months every tire blow-out
was final, every strange car near the house
kept watch and I strained even to remember
things impossible to forget. You took
my stories apart for hours, sitting
on your sofa with your legs under you
and fifty years in your face.
                So you know
now, you said, what kind of money
is involved and that *campesinos* knife
one another and you know you should
not trust anyone and so you find a few
people you will trust. You know the mix
of machetes with whiskey, the slip of the tongue
that costs hundreds of deaths.
You've seen the pits where men and women
are kept the few days it takes without
food and water. You've heard the cocktail
conversation on which their release depends.
So you've come to understand why
men and women of good will read
torture reports with fascination.

Such things as water pumps
and co-op farms are of little importance
and take years.
It is not Che Guevara, this struggle.
Camillo Torres is dead. Victor Jara
was rounded up with the others, and José
Martí is a landing strip for planes
from Miami to Cuba. Go try on
Americans your long, dull story
of corruption, but better to give
them what they want: Lil Milagro Ramirez,
who after years of confinement did not
know what year it was, how she walked
with help and was forced to shit in public.
Tell them about the razor, the live wire,
dry ice and concrete, grey rats and above all
who fucked her, how many times and when.
Tell them about retaliation: José lying
on the flat bed truck, waving his stumps
in your face, his hands cut off by his
captors and thrown to the many acres
of cotton, lost, still, and holding
the last few lumps of leeched earth.
Tell them of José in his last few hours
and later how, many months later,
a labor leader was cut to pieces and buried.
Tell them how his friends found
the soldiers and made them dig him up
and ask forgiveness of the corpse, once
it was assembled again on the ground
like a man. As for the cars, of course
they watch you and for this don't flatter
yourself. We are all watched. We are
all assembled.

Josephine, I tell you
I have not rested, not since I drove
those streets with a gun in my lap,
not since all manner of speaking has
failed and the remnant of my life
continues onward. I go mad, for example,
in the Safeway, at the many heads
of lettuce, papayas and sugar, pineapples
and coffee, especially the coffee.
And when I speak with American men,
there is some absence of recognition:
their constant Scotch and fine white
hands, many hours of business, penises
hardened by motor inns and a faint
resemblance to their wives. I cannot
keep going. I remember the American
attaché in that country: his tanks
of fish, his clicking pen, his rapt
devotion to reports. His wife wrote
his reports. She said as much as she
gathered him each day from the embassy
compound, that she was tired of covering
up, sick of his drinking and the loss
of his last promotion. She was a woman
who flew her own plane, stalling out
after four martinis to taxi on an empty
field in the *campo* and to those men
and women announce she was there to help.
She flew where she pleased in that country
with her drunken kindness, while Marines
in white gloves were assigned to protect
her husband. It was difficult work, what
with the suspicion on the rise in smaller

countries that gringos die like other men.
I cannot, Josephine, talk to them.

And so, you say, you've learned a little
about starvation: a child like a supper scrap
filling with worms, many children strung
together, as if they were cut from paper
and all in a delicate chain. And that people
who rescue physicists, lawyers and poets
lie in their beds at night with reports
of mice introduced into women, of men
whose testicles are crushed like eggs.
That they cup their own parts
with their bedsheets and move themselves
slowly, imagining bracelets affixing
their wrists to a wall where the naked
are pinned, where the naked are tied open
and left to the hands of those who erase
what they touch. We are all erased
by them, and no longer resemble decent
men. We no longer have the hearts,
the strength, the lives of women.
Your problem is not your life as it is
in America, not that your hands, as you
tell me, are tied to do something. It is
that you were born to an island of greed
and grace where you have this sense
of yourself as apart from others. It is
not your right to feel powerless. Better
people than you were powerless.
You have not returned to your country,
but to a life you never left.

1980

20

MESSAGE

YOUR voices sprayed over the walls
dry to the touch by morning.
Your women walk among *champas*
with baskets of live hens, grenades and fruit.
Tonight you begin to fight
for the most hopeless of revolutions.
Pedro, you place a host on each
man's chant of *Body of Christ Amen*.
Margarita, you slip from your house
with plastiques wrapped in newsprint,
the dossier of your dearest friend
whose hair grew to the floor of her cell.
Leonel, you load your bare few guns
with an idea for a water pump and
co-operative farm.
                    You will fight
and fighting, you will die. I will live
and living cry out until my voice is gone
to its hollow of earth, where with our
hands and by the lives we have chosen
we will dig deep into our deaths.
I have done all that I could do.
Link hands, link arms with me
in the next of lives everafter,
where we will not know each other
or ourselves, where we will be a various
darkness among ideas that amounted
to nothing, among men who amounted

to nothing, with a belief that became
but small light
in the breadth of time where we began
among each other, where we lived
in the hour farthest from God.

1980–81

BECAUSE ONE IS ALWAYS FORGOTTEN

IN MEMORIAM, JOSÉ RUDOLFO VIERA
1939–1981: EL SALVADOR

WHEN Viera was buried we knew it had come to an end,
his coffin rocking into the ground like a boat or a cradle.

I could take my heart, he said, and give it to a *campesino*
and he would cut it up and give it back:

you can't eat heart in those four dark
chambers where a man can be kept years.

A boy soldier in the bone-hot sun works his knife
to peel the face from a dead man

and hang it from the branch of a tree
flowering with such faces.

The heart is the toughest part of the body.
Tenderness is in the hands.

RENION

Of all the things I did and all the things I said
Let no one try to find out who I was
An obstacle was there transforming
The actions and the manner of my life
An obstacle was often there
To silence me when I began to speak

CONSTANTINE P. CAVAFY

ENDURANCE

In Belgrade, the windows of the tourist
hotel opened over seven storeys of lilacs,
rain clearing sidewalk tables of linens
and liquor, the silk flags of the non-
aligned nations like colorful underthings
pinned to the wind. Tito was living.
I bought English, was mistaken for Czech,
walked to the fountains, the market
of garlic and tents, where I saw
my dead Anna again and again,
hard yellow beans in her lap,
her babushka of white summer cotton,
her eyes the hard pits of her past.
She was gossiping among her friends,
saying the rosary or trying to sell me
something. Anna. Peeling her hands
with a paring knife, saying *in your country
you have nothing.* Each word was the husk
of a vegetable tossed to the street
or a mountain rounded by trains
with cargoes of sheep-dung and grief.
I searched in Belgrade for some holy
face painted *without hands* as when
an ikon painter goes to sleep and awakens
with an image come from the dead.
On each corner Anna dropped
her work in her lap and looked up.
I am a childless poet, I said.

I have not painted an egg, made prayers
or finished my Easter duty in years.
I left Belgrade for Frankfurt last
summer, Frankfurt for New York,
New York for the Roanoke valley
where mountains hold the breath
of the dead between them and lift
from each morning a fresh bandage of mist.
New York, Roanoke, the valley—
to this Cape where in the dunes
the wind takes a body of its own
and a fir tree comes to the window
at night, tapping on the glass like
a woman who has lived too much.
Piskata, hold your tongue, she says.
I am trying to tell you something.

EXPATRIATE

AMERICAN life, you said, is not possible.
Winter in Syracuse, Trotsky pinned
to your kitchen wall, windows facing
a street, boxes of imported cigarettes.
The film *In the Realm of the Senses*,
and piles of shit burning and the risk
of having your throat slit. Twenty-year-old poet.
To be in love with some woman who cannot speak
English, to have her soften your back with oil
and beat on your mattress with grief and pleasure
as you take her from behind, moving beneath you
like the beginning of the world.
The black smell of death as blood and glass
is hosed from the street and the beggar holds
his diminishing hand to your face.
It would be good if you could wind up
in prison and so write your prison poems.
Good if you could marry the veiled face
and jewelled belly of a girl who could
cook Turkish meat, baste your body
with a wet and worshipful tongue.
Istanbul, you said, or *Serbia*, mauve
light and mystery and passing for other
than American, a *Kalishnikov* over
your shoulder, spraying your politics
into the flesh of an enemy become real.
You have been in Turkey a year now.
What have you found? Your letters

describe the boring ritual of tea,
the pittance you are paid to teach
English, the bribery required for so much
as a postage stamp. Twenty-year-old poet,
Hikmet did not choose to be Hikmet.

LETTER FROM PRAGUE, 1968–78

It is winter again, those cold
globes of breath that shape
themselves into bodies. I am still
in prison having bowls of paste
for breakfast; I wake
to the bath of lights in the yard,
the violent shadow of a man running
as I should have run,
as I should have climbed, leaving
the moons of my fingers where
no one would find them.
It is ten years and hard
to believe even now that in
1968 I should have been
so stupid, touching my glass
to a soldier's saying *viva
Dubcek, viva svoboda, viva
socialisme*. At twenty-eight
I am old, recalling bottles
we filled with gasoline
corked with rags from our
mothers' dresses, and that slow
word *soviet* spoken on a stream
of spit. I could have
fallen in love. There were
plenty of women in the streets
calling *roses, roses*; I should
have given them money, taken

their petals to a room where
I might have dropped to a bed,
my eyes tongued open at morning.
To touch myself now, there is nothing.

DEPARTURE

WE take it with us, the cry
of a train slicing a field
leaving its stiff suture, a distant
tenderness as when rails slip
behind us and our windows
touch the field, where it seems
the dead are awake and so reach
for each other. Your hand
cups the light of a match
to your mouth, to mine, and I want
to ask if the dead hold
their mouths in their hands like this
to know what is left of them.
Between us, a tissue of smoke,
a bundle of belongings, luggage
that will seem to float beside us,
the currency we will change
and change again. Here is the name
of a friend who will take you in,
the papers of a man who vanished,
the one you will become when
the man you have been disappears.
I am the woman whose photograph
you will not recognize, whose face
emptied your eyes, whose eyes
were brief, like the smallest
of cities we slipped through.

PHOTOGRAPH OF MY ROOM

after Walker Evans

THIRTY years from now, you might
hold this room in your hands.
So that you will not wonder:
the china cups are from Serbia
where a man filled them with plum
wine and one night talked
of his life with the partisans
and in prison, his life
as a poet, Slavko, his life
as if it could not have been otherwise.
The quilt was Anna's.
There are swatches taken
from her own clothes, curtains
that hung in a kitchen in Prague,
aprons she never took off
in all her years in America.
Since her death, the stitches,
one scrap to another
have come loose.

The bundle of army letters
were sent from Southeast Asia
during '67, kept near a bottle
of vodka drained by a woman
in that same year who wanted
only to sleep; the fatigues

were his, it is she
whom I now least resemble.

In the trunk, the white eyelet
and cheap lace of underthings,
a coat that may have belonged
to a woman who approached me
on a street in April
saying, as it was spring,
would I spare her a smoke?

Under the bed, a pouch of money:
pesetas, dinar, francs, the coins
of no value in any other place.
In the notebooks you will find
those places: the damp inner thighs,
the delicate rash left by kisses,
fingers on the tongue, a swallow
of brandy, a fire.
It is all there, the lies
told to myself because of Paris,
the stories I believed in Salvador
and Granada, and every so often
simply the words calling back
a basket of lemons and eggs,
a bowl of olives.

Wrapped in a tissue you will find
a bullet, as if from the rifle
on the wall, spooned from the flesh
of a friend who must have thought
it was worth something.
Latched to its shell, a lattice
of muscle. *One regime*

is like another said the face
of a doctor who slid
the bullet from the flat
of his blade to my hands saying
this one won't live to the morning.

In the black cheese crock
are the ashes, flecked
with white slivers of bone,
that should have been scattered
years ago, but the thing
did not seem possible.
The rest of the room remains
a mystery, as it was
in the shutter of memory
that was 1936, when it belonged
to someone already dead, someone
who has no belongings.

ON RETURNING TO DETROIT

OVER the plum snow, the train's blonde smoke,
dawn coming into Detroit but like Bratislava

the icy undersides of the train, the passengers
asleep on one another and those who cannot

pace the aisles touching seats to steady themselves
and between the cars their hair is silvered

by the fine ice that covers everything; a man
slamming his hand into a morning paper

a woman who has so rubbed her bright grey eyes
during grief that all she has seen can be seen in them

the century, of which twenty years are left,
several wars, a fire of black potatoes

and maybe a moment when across a table
she was loved and as a much younger woman

wet her fingertip and played the bells of empty
glasses of wine, impossible not to imagine her

doing that, drawing the shade and then in its ochre
light, the first button of his shirt, the rest

the plants boarded up along the wide black river,
the spools of unraveling light that are the rails

the domed Greek church, the glass hopes of the city
beside one another; the man whose clothes

he carries in a pillowcase, the woman whose old love
walks into her eyes each morning and with a pole

lowers the awnings over the shop stalls of fruit.

AS CHILDREN TOGETHER

UNDER the sloped snow
pinned all winter with Christmas
lights, we waited for your father
to whittle his soap cakes
away, finish the whisky,
your mother to carry her coffee
from room to room closing lights
cubed in the snow at our feet.
Holding each other's
coat sleeves we slid down
the roads in our tight
black dresses, past
crystal swamps and the death
face of each dark house,
over the golden ice
of tobacco spit, the blue
quiet of ponds, with town
glowing behind the blind
white hills and a scant
snow ticking in the stars.
You hummed *blanche comme
la neige* and spoke of Montreal
where a *quebeçoise* could sing,
take any man's face
to her unfastened blouse
and wake to wine
on the bedside table.
I always believed this,

Victoria, that there might
be a way to get out.

You were ashamed of that house,
its round tins of surplus flour,
chipped beef and white beans,
relief checks and winter trips
that always ended in deer
tied stiff to the car rack,
the accordion breath of your uncles
down from the north, and what
you called the stupidity
of the Michigan French.

Your mirror grew ringed
with photos of servicemen
who had taken your breasts
in their hands, the buttons
of your blouses in their teeth,
who had given you the silk
tassles of their graduation,
jackets embroidered with dragons
from the Far East. You kept
the corks that had fired
from bottles over their beds,
their letters with each city
blackened, envelopes of hair
from their shaved heads.

I am going to have it, you said.
Flowers wrapped in paper from carts
in Montreal, a plane lifting out
of Detroit, a satin bed, a table
cluttered with bottles of scent.

So standing in a platter of ice
outside a Catholic dance hall
you took their collars
in your fine chilled hands
and lied your age to adulthood.

I did not then have breasts of my own,
nor any letters from bootcamp
and when one of the men who had
gathered around you took my mouth
to his own there was nothing
other than the dance hall music
rising to the arms of iced trees.

I don't know where you are now, Victoria.
They say you have children, a trailer
in the snow near our town,
and the husband you found as a girl
returned from the Far East broken
cursing holy blood at the table
where nightly a pile of white shavings
is paid from the edge of his knife.

If you read this poem, write to me.
I have been to Paris since we parted.

JOSEPH

This is the moment you have
to yourself, the slip of your knife
along the windshield, the smoke
of your breath when
on black winter mornings
you make your sack of sausage and apple.
You walk where my father walked.
You follow your brothers
into the spray of stars that is
a steel mill, past the green high
windows of the steel mill in summer
and the long benches for lunch.
This is the table where you make
your bullets and line them up
fine and golden as siloes
in Dakota, bullets from which
the empty tin cans will pass daylight.
It is a jeep almost paid for,
a woman who comes home with you
from a long bar night of smoke and poker.
You take her panties to your face
and it is all you have and all
your father had and all your brothers.
With you they dip their lines
to that silent and promising
water of summer, hoping
as they hoped for more than fish.
So you are worried about your life.

Your voice carries across state lines,
over the crispened fields of winter
fodder, where snow hovers over wheat
like moths, where moths hover.
Your voice in its wrapper of ice
blue with the breath of cupped hands.
After ten years you want
so fervently to talk about the war
like those who have gone to war before you.
I listen to the cries that kill
for meat, rabbits ripped from their furs,
deer taken, as birds drop through
an emptiness of swamp, as snakes
unfurl from a coil that is final.
And then, you say, the fry pan
where something is lifted from
pan to plate within you,
the fragment of fire within you.
the boy from Iowa who held your leg
and cried into your pants for his home,
until the chopper wind of an evacuation
carried him out of your arms.
You speak now of the accurate
ballistics tables, the morning
when we were called home,
the years it took to kiss me.
You say your palms are now
whiskered with steel from
the flickering remnants of your work.
It is no life for you, Joseph.
It is not enough, the fish,
the white heads of beer, your winnings.
When we were young it was
other than that, your thighs

through waist-high fields,
your nets closing on cabbage moths,
the small rocks where the early life
of the world was pressed forever,
the jars where all that was trapped
crawled and the pond life trembled.
There were storeys of light
in the clouds, an afterlife, songs
to God from the open windows of our
rooms where at night without one
another, we touched.
Now this feel of knife for fish,
of bullet for something racing through
the darkness, your voice
slung on the wires that lapse
scalloping the cold length
of the country between us.
It is another voice that calls me
after all this time.
It has nothing to say to you, Joseph.

SELECTIVE SERVICE

WE rise from the snow where we've
lain on our backs and flown like children,
from the imprint of perfect wings and cold gowns,
and we stagger together wine-breathed into town
where our people are building
their armies again, short years after
body bags, after burnings. There is a man
I've come to love after thirty, and we have
our rituals of coffee, of airports, regret.
After love we smoke and sleep
with magazines, two shot glasses
and the black and white collapse of hours.
In what time do we live that it is too late
to have children? In what place
that we consider the various ways to leave?
There is no list long enough
for a selective service card shriveling
under a match, the prison that comes of it,
a flag in the wind eaten from its pole
and boys sent back in trash bags.
We'll tell you. You were at that time
learning fractions. We'll tell you
about fractions. Half of us are dead or quiet
or lost. Let them speak for themselves
We lie down in the fields and leave behind
the corpses of angels.

FOR THE STRANGER

ALTHOUGH you mention Venice
keeping it on your tongue like a fruit pit
and I say yes, perhaps Bucharest, neither of us
really knows. There is only this train
slipping through pastures of snow,
a sleigh reaching down
to touch its buried runners.
We meet on the shaking platform,
the wind's broken teeth sinking into us.
You unwrap your dark bread
and share with me the coffee
sloshing into your gloves.
Telegraph posts chop the winter fields
into white blocks, in each window
the crude painting of a small farm.
We listen to mothers scolding
children in English as if
we do not understand a word of it—
sit still, sit still.

There are few clues as to where
we are: the baled wheat scattered
everywhere like missing coffins.
The distant yellow kitchen lights
wiped with oil.
Everywhere the black dipping wires
stretching messages from one side
of a country to the other.

The men who stand on every border
waving to us.

Wiping ovals of breath from the windows
in order to see ourselves, you touch
the glass tenderly wherever it holds my face.
Days later, you are showing me
photographs of a woman and children
smiling from the windows of your wallet.

Each time the train slows, a man
with our faces in the gold buttons
of his coat passes through the cars
muttering the name of a city. Each time
we lose people. Each time I find you
again between the cars, holding out
a scrap of bread for me, something
hot to drink, until there are
no more cities and you pull me
toward you, sliding your hands
into my coat, telling me
your name over and over, hurrying
your mouth into mine.
We have, each of us, nothing.
We will give it to each other.

REUNION

Just as he changes himself, in the end
eternity changes him.

MALLARMÉ

ON the phonograph, the voice
of a woman already dead for three
decades, singing of a man
who could make her do anything.
On the table, two fragile
glasses of black wine,
a bottle wrapped in its towel.
It is that room, the one
we took in every city, it is
as I remember: the bed, a block
of moonlight and pillows.
My fingernails, pecks of light
on your thighs.
The stink of the fire escape.
The wet butts of cigarettes
you crushed one after another.
How I watched the morning come
as you slept, more my son
than a man ten years older.
How my breasts feel, years
later, the tongues swishing
in my dress, some yours, some
left by other men.
Since then, I have always

wakened first, I have learned
to leave a bed without being
seen and have stood
at the washbasins, wiping oil
and salt from my skin,
staring at the cupped water
in my two hands.
I have kept everything
you whispered to me then.
I can remember it now as I see you
again, how much tenderness we could
wedge between a stairwell
and a police lock, or as it was,
as it still is, in the voice
of a woman singing of a man
who could make her do anything.

CITY WALK-UP, WINTER 1969

THERE is the morning shuffle of traffic confined
to a window, the blue five p.m. of a street
light, a yellow supper left untouched.
A previous month is pinned to the wall where
days are numbered differently and described by
the photograph of a dead season. If I could
move from the bed I would clear the window
and cold-palmed watch myself at twenty, walking
in frozen socks with sacks of clothes and letters,
wearing three winter coats from Goodwill,
keeping a footing on the slick silence
of the hysterical deaf. When I tell of my life
now it is not this version.

I would see her climb three flights
of a condemned house with her bags
because she is still awakened
by a wrecking ball swung to the attic ribs
and the shelled daylight that followed her
everywhere after that: a silent implosion
of rooms, the xylophone bells as a fire
escape plummeted toward the ice.
Even now the house itself is etched
on the hard black air where it had been.
No one knew about it then: meals
of raw egg and snow, rolls of insulation
in which she wrapped herself, a blanket
of brown paper and spun glass.

From Kosinski she took the idea of a tin
can, its white lard given to birds, small
holes of punched light on her face.
She wrote names on walls and was aware
of her hands, chewing the skin into small
white scraps around each nail. She still
eats her hands and steals bread: street
screamer, housewife, supermarket thief.

We do not rid ourselves of these things
even when we are cured of personal silence
when for no reason one morning
we begin to hear the noise of the world again.

POEM FOR MAYA

DIPPING our bread in oil tins
we talked of morning peeling
open our rooms to a moment
of almonds, olives and wind
when we did not yet know what we were.
The days in Mallorca were alike:
footprints down goat-paths
from the beds we had left,
at night the stars locked to darkness.
At that time we were learning
to dance, take our clothes
in our fingers and open
ourselves to their hands.
The *veranera* was with us.
For a month the almond trees bloomed,
their droppings the delicate silks
we removed when each time a touch
took us closer to the window where
we whispered *yes*, there on the intricate
balconies of breath, overlooking
the rest of our lives.

III

OURSELVES OR NOTHING

OURSELVES OR NOTHING

FOR TERRENCE DE PRES

AFTER seven years and as the wine
leaves and black trunks of maples wait
beyond the window, I think of you
north, in the few lighted rooms
of that ruined house, a candle in each
open pane of breath, the absence of anyone,
snow in a hurry to earth, my fingernails
pressing half moons into the sill
as I watched you pouring three
then four fingers of Scotch over ice,
the chill in your throat like a small
blue bone, those years of your work
on the Holocaust. You had to walk
off the darkness, miles of winter
riverfront, windows the eyes in skulls
along the river, gratings in the streets
over jewelled human sewage, your breath
hanging about your face like tobacco.
I was with you even then, your face
the face of a clock as you swept
through the memoirs of men and women
who would not give up. In the short light
of Decembers, you took suppers of whole
white hens and pans of broth
in a city of liquor bottles and light.
Go after that which is lost
and all the mass graves of the century's dead

will open into your early waking hours:
Belsen, Dachau, Saigon, Phnom Penh
and the one meaning Bridge of Ravens,
Sao Paulo, Armagh, Calcutta, Salvador,
although these are not the same.
You wrote too of Theresienstadt,
that word that ran screaming into
my girlhood, lifting its grey wool dress,
the smoke in its violent plumes and feathers,
the dark wormy heart of the human desire to die.
In Prague, Anna told me, there was bread,
stubborn potatoes and fish, armies and the women
who lie down with them, eggs perhaps but never
meat, never meat but the dead.
In Theresienstadt she said there was only the dying.
Never bread, potatoes, fish or women.
They were all as yet girls then.
Vast numbers of men and women died, you wrote,
because they did not have time, the blessing
of sheer time, to recover. Your ration of time
was smaller then, a tin spoon of winter,
piano notes one at a time from the roof
to the gutter. I am only imagining this,
as I had not yet entered your life
like the dark fact of a gun on your pillow,
or Anna Akhmatova's "Requiem"
and its final *I can* when the faceless woman
before her asked *can you describe this?*
I was not yet in your life when you turned
the bullet toward the empty hole in yourself
and whispered: finish this or die.
But you lived and what you wrote became
The Survivor, that act of contrition for despair:
They turned to face the worst

straight-on, without sentiment or hope,
simply to keep watch over life. Now,
as you sleep face down on your papers,
the book pages turning of themselves
in your invisible breath, I climb
the stairs of that house, fragile
with age and the dry fear of burning
and I touch the needle to music to wake you,
the snow long past falling, something
by Vivaldi or Brahms.
I have come from our cacophonous
ordinary lives where I stood at the sink
last summer scrubbing mud from potatoes
and listening to the supper fish
in the skillet, my eyes on the narrowed
streets of rain through the window
as I thought of the long war
that misted country turned to the moon's surface,
grey and ring-wormed with ridges of light.
the women in their silk *ao dais* along
the river, those flowers under fire, rolled
at night in the desperate arms of American men.
Once I walked your rooms with my
nightdress open, a cigarette from my lips
to the darkness and back as you worked
at times through to the morning.
Always on my waking you were gone,
the blue holes of your path through snow
to the road, your face still haggard
in the white mirror, the pained note
where ten times you had written
the word *recalcitrance* and once:
you will die and live
under the name of someone

who has actually died.
I think of that night in a tropic hotel,
the man who danced with a tray over his head
and offered us free because we were *socialistas*,
not only that, he sang, but young and pretty.
Later as I lay on a cot in the heat naked
my friend was able to reach for the guns
and load them clicking in the moonlight
with only the barest of sounds;
he had heard them before me moving among the palms.
We were going to die there.
I remember the moon notching its way
through the palms and the calm sense that came
for me at the end of my life. In that moment
the woman beside me became my sister,
her hand cupping her mouth, the blood
that would later spill from her face
if what we believed were the truth.
Her blood would crawl black and belly-down
onto a balcony of hands and flashlights,
cameras, flowers, propaganda.
Her name was René and without knowing
her you wrote: *all things human take time,*
time which the damned never have, time for life
to repair at least the worst of its wounds;
it took time to wake, time for horror
to incite revolt, time for the recovery
of lucidity and will.
In the late afternoons you returned,
the long teeth shining from the eaves,
a clink in the wood half-burnt
and as you touched it alive:
ici repose un déporté inconnu.
In the mass graves, a woman's hand

caged in the ribs of her child,
a single stone in Spain beneath olives,
in Germany the silent windy fields,
in the Soviet Union where the snow
is scarred with wire, in Salvador
where the blood will never soak
into the ground, everywhere and always
go after that which is lost.
There is a cyclone fence between
ourselves and the slaughter and behind it
we hover in a calm protected world like
netted fish, exactly like netted fish.
It is either the beginning or the end
of the world, and the choice is ourselves
or nothing.